The Act Unpacked

The Meaning of the 1988 Education Reform Act for Religious Education

John M Hull

Birmingham Papers in Religious Education No 1.
The University of Birmingham and the Christian Education Movement 1989.

Birmingham Papers in Religious Education are edited jointly by the University of Birmingham School of Education and the Christian Education Movement.

ABOUT CEM

The Christian Education Movement is a charitable foundation which, among other things, provides support for Religious Education in schools. It is funded partly by grants from local education authorities, and the Council of Local Education Authorities recommends its members to subscribe to CEM. Other sources of finance include grants from trusts and from the churches, and CEM also generates its own income through subscriptions and the sale of publications. It offers advisory services, runs conferences for both teachers and pupils, and provides high quality resources for Religious Education through its subscription services and publications catalogue. To receive further details, including the current catalogue, send to the address below.

CEM,
P.O. Box 36
ISLEWORTH
Middlesex
TW7 5DE

ISBN 1 85100 060 7

CONTENTS

Contents

INTRODUCTION

Although the 1988 Education Reform Act contains much that is new in religious education, it also suggests continuity. In what follows we shall distinguish between elements of change and elements of continuity, and draw attention to some points where the Act is a little ambiguous. We shall deal first with religious education as a subject of the curriculum. Next, we shall consider what the Act has to say about the religious life of the school as a whole. Finally, we shall consider how the Act affects the administration of religion in schools.

No attempt is made to describe every detail mentioned in the Act, but attention is concentrated upon what is most important for the place of religion and religious education in school life. Those who need to check on the details of how SACREs work will need to consult the Act itself. It is hoped, however, that members of SACREs, governors, parents, teachers and anyone interested in religion in our schools will find in what follows a useful guide.

School of Education
University of Birmingham
November 20th 1988

Chapter 1

RELIGIOUS EDUCATION AS A SUBJECT OF THE CURRICULUM

1. Religious Education becomes more educational

The first thing to notice is that the subject is no longer described as "religious instruction" but as "religious education". In Sec.1:1 we read that the various educational authorities are "to exercise their functions ...with respect to religious education, religious worship and the National Curriculum".[1] The curriculum for every maintained school shall comprise "a basic curriculum which includes (a) provision for religious education for all registered pupils at the school ..."(2:1).

Thomas Arnold (1795-1842) of Rugby School was one of the pioneers of the distinction between religious instruction and religious education. Religious instruction was no more than the teaching of catechisms, hymns and the main principles and facts of religion and could only give somebody a map of the way. Religious education, however, helped one to travel the road. It implied the formation of the whole person and could only be effective if the ideal permeated the whole of school life.[2] By the 1920s there was no longer any doubt. "Religious education is something more than religious instruction".[3] "Education is the nurturing of the whole personality".[4] Thus instruction was thought of as the cognitive or didactic heart of a larger process of humanisation.

By the 1930s leaders of religious education were calling for a change in the official terminology, which still retained "religious instruction". Dr Basil Yeaxlee wrote "Some of us have developed a loathing for the word instruction - so much so we avoid using it ...".[5] He complains that authorities at Whitehall and elsewhere insist upon using the word instruction when what is meant is education. "...we revolt against the apparent reduction of the greater and more generous to the less and the more formal. ... there is something desiccating and deadening in referring always to religious education as religious instruction".[6] There was a sense, Yeaxlee remarked, in which the continued use of the expression "religious instruction" was nothing more than "an amusing foible of officialdom".[7]

In spite of this, "religious instruction" was retained in 1944, but this did reflect one aspect of current usage. Religious education referred to the whole (i.e. instruction plus worship) while "religious instruction" referred to the part (i.e. the classroom teaching only). This was consistent with the idea that religious education was greater than religious instruction, while retaining the idea that the imparting of knowledge was a central feature of it. In the years immediately following, however, the meanings of the terms continued to evolve, and it is notable that many of the agreed syllabuses were now describing themselves as "religious education".

In 1947 Professor T. E. Jessop reviewed the impact of the war upon the processes of adult education. Far too many men, it had been discovered, had no intellectual resources except propaganda to combat propaganda itself. An understanding of the ideals of democracy needed to be built up through a more truly educative process. Jessop describes how the Armed Forces set in motion a programme of education which included religious education. The Army chaplains were encouraged to adopt styles of teaching rather than preaching, to invite criticism and to provoke discussion. "... the educational way rests on a deep respect for personality. Its ideal is the enlargement, integration and maturing of this. Its method is therefore a constant care of the faculties ...the widening of imagination, the enhancement of the power of seeking truth and discerning it ...".[8]

By the 1960s there was an active search for a fully educational rationale for the place of religion in the school curriculum. An influential example of this may be found in the contribution by F. H. Hilliard to the 1965 Hibbert Lectures. The task of religious education is to make a contribution to the quest on the part of young people for a faith by which to live although this may or may not be found in the faith which was usually presented, ie in the main Christianity. Other world religions together with secular alternatives to religion should also be presented. Religious education should not seek to advance the cause of Christian faith in any direct manner, let alone try to create church members.[9] The influential article by Edwin Cox "Educational Religious Education" was published in 1971,[10] and it was only sensitivity to legal pressure which caused the makers of the 1975 City of Birmingham Agreed Syllabus to call it an "Agreed Syllabus of Religious Instruction".

The 1988 Education Reform Act finally abandons the instructional vocabulary and refers to the subject as religious education. This comes as no surprise, but rather as a long overdue recognition of the educational responsibilities which lie upon the teacher of religion in maintained schools. The history of the terms shows that religious education was preferred to instruction because it described a deeper and richer process of human development. Processes such as Christian evangelisation and Christian nurture, to say nothing of indoctrination, were gradually distinguished from religious education. To be educated was to have a certain sense of perspective, a quality of independent judgement, together with a wide grasp of the cultural traditions, everything which is summed up so well in the introduction to the 1988 Act when it is said that the curriculum of the maintained school shall be a "balanced and broadly based curriculum which promotes the spiritual, moral, cultural, mental and physical development of pupils at the school and of society..."(Sec 1:2). In finally abandoning its instructional legacy, religious education thus finds parliamentary support in making a contribution to the spirituality and to the cultural traditions, everything which is summed up so well in the introduction to the 1988 Act when it is said that the curriculum of the maintained school shall be a "balanced and broadly based curriculum which promotes the spiritual, moral, cultural, mental and physical development of pupils at the school and of society..."(Sec 1:2). In finally abandoning its instructional legacy, religious education thus finds parliamentary support in making a contribution to the spirituality and to the cultural traditions of society. The contribution of religious education is to be broader and more balanced in the mental and moral areas, and this is to be interpreted developmentally, both in the case of the individual pupil and for society at large. Society as a whole, through such a curriculum, is to become broader and more balanced.

The educational nature of the approach endorsed by the new Act is underlined by the interesting revision of the Cowper-Temple clause (Section 26:2 of the 1944 Act as amended 1988). This clause was first introduced in the 1870 Forster Act to prevent the teaching of religion in schools taking a denominational form, and so religious education was not to be given "by means of any catechism or formulary which is distinctive of any particular religious denomination". When an educational rather than an instructional or a proselytizing approach is taken, however, it is the distinctive features of a religious group which make it interesting. There is no point in learning about Methodism unless one learns what is distinctive of Methodism. The revised 1988 form of the clause thus continues: "but this provision is not to be taken as prohibiting provision in such a syllabus for *the study of* such catechisms or formularies" (emphasis added). The concept of religious studies is thus included in the new legislation.

We must thus interpret the 1988 Education Reform Act as expressing the continuity and the natural fulfilment of the trend which we have been describing. It is in the light of this that we must interpret everything which the Act says about religion, whether in the classroom, in the school as a whole or in the administrative procedures. The essential questions which we must always ask of religion in our schools are these. Is it behaving in a way which is truly educational? Is it tending towards balance and broadness? Is it enhancing the moral and mental development of pupils and of society? Is it deepening the human qualities of children and young people by encouraging an independent quest for the truth and, at the same time, transmitting a broadly based and balanced understanding of the religious traditions of humanity?[11]

2. Religious education in the basic curriculum

Having in its preliminary comments prepared us for the more broadly based and balanced role which religious education, strengthened in its educational nature, is to play, the Act now introduces the concept of the basic curriculum. It is, perhaps, a pity that Sec.2 of the Act is introduced by the heading "The National Curriculum" since 2:1 goes on immediately to say that "the curriculum for every maintained school shall comprise a basic curriculum which includes (a) provision for religious education for all registered pupils at the school; and (b) a curriculum for all registered pupils at the school of compulsory school age (to be known as the National Curriculum ...)". The "basic curriculum" is thus more comprehensive than the "National Curriculum" and the heading should have referred the reader to the whole not merely to part of it. Be that as it may, the essential point is that everything in the National Curriculum is also in the basic curriculum but the reverse is not the case. Religious education is unique in being basic but not national. Everything in the curriculum which the Act prescribes is basic but only the core and other foundation subjects are national. Why is this?

Religious education in England and Wales already occupied a situation of unique balance between national and local interests. Under the 1944 Act it was the only subject of the curriculum which was required by national law, and was also the only subject for which special local curriculum arrangements were in force. Under the agreed syllabuses, which arose in the 1920s and 30s and were given parliamentary support in the 1944 Act, parents through their elected councillors, and teachers through their unions, had direct influence upon what the schools taught. This represented an important recognition of the centrality of this subject in commuity life. It was the community which negotiated its own religious education. This represented a unique degree of accountability in the curriculum, and there is no doubt that in this respect religious education was something of a model subject. It must also be emphasized that although its national status made religious education, in a sense, the only compulsory subject, it was also, in an equally significant sense, the only optional subject, since parents had the right in this but in no other subject of the curriculum to opt their children out.

This freedom for genuine sensitivity to the community has been strengthened by the 1988 Act, and we will return to this when we consider the administration of the subject. At this point, it is necessary only that we take note of the important realignment of the relationship between local and national interests which the new Act prescribes.

The powers of central government are severely limited in the case of religious education, and in the case of religious education only. When we turn to the National Curriculum, virtually the only thing which the Secretary of State for Education cannot change is his responsibility for the provision of some national curriculum or other, and that it should specify "attainment targets", "programmes of study" and "assessment arrangements" for each subject within each "key stage" of schooling. Moreover, the National Curriculum must be organised into "core and other foundation subjects". All of that is in Sec.2 and is beyond the power of the Secretary of State to change. After that, however, his power is virtually unlimited. Although Sec.3 says that the core subjects shall be Mathematics, English, and Science, together with Welsh in Welsh speaking schools, and that the other foundation subjects shall be History, Geography, Technology, Music, Art and Physical Education, together with Welsh in schools in Wales which are not Welsh speaking, and in the secondary school only, a foreign language, the Secretary of State can change all this. That is made perfectly clear in Sec.4. The Secretary of State may bring foundation subjects in or out of the core, he may drop subjects altogether, or introduce new ones. He can "revise that Curriculum whenever he considers it necessary or expedient to do so" (Sec.4:1(b)). It is his responsibility to determine the programmes of study which each of the National Curriculum subjects shall offer. He cannot, however, drop religious education; he cannot determine its programmes of study or add anything whatever to its objectives, which remain only as stated in Sec.1, namely, that religious education like the rest of the basic curriculum shall contribute to the spiritual, moral, cultural, mental and physical development of the pupil and of society, and shall be broadly based and balanced. The Secretary of State can have no views as to why or what pupils shall learn in religious education.

We can now see that religious education is more basic than the rest of the basic curriculum. It is there by Act of Parliament and is not subject to the powers of the Secretary of State.

Subject to some important sections of the Act which we shall discuss shortly, religious education remains a local matter, just as it did before. Each local education authority is to convene a "conference" which has the responsibility of adopting an agreed syllabus for the maintained schools within its jurisdiction. We may thus say that religious education is more basic in that it is closer to the grass roots. It is the only required area of the curriculum over which local people including parents and teachers have control.

Finally, religious education is more basic in that it is, of all the subjects, the one most closely related to the first of the principal characteristics which the whole curriculum is to have, namely, the spiritual, and it is accordingly the first subject in the basic curriculum to be mentioned. Similarly, in the opening statements of the Act where the principal duties of the educational authorities, whether the Secretary of State, the local education authorities or the governors and heads of schools, are being described, their first responsibility is for religious education and religious worship, and only after that is their responsibility for the National Curriculum mentioned.

6

Although agreed syllabuses for religious education remain a local responsibility, the 1988 Act introduces a new requirement which has the effect of widening the perspective of local communities. In drawing up its agreed syllabus, a local conference is required to consider not the local religious situation but that of Great Britain. This is emphasized at several points in the Act and its full significance will be discussed below. At present, it is sufficient for us to notice that the requirement to survey the religious characteristics of Great Britain as a whole will from now on prevent agreed syllabuses from becoming parochial. It has been traditional for them to include material on, for example, how Christianity came to Wiltshire. Such materials may or may not be included in any new agreed syllabuses drawn up under the provisions of the 1988 Act, but one thing is clear: the horizons of these agreed syllabuses must go beyond the boundaries of the county and, indeed, the nation. Agreed syllabuses in England may not confine their contents to the religious situation in England, just as the Welsh provision will not fulfil the requirement of the Act if it is confined to the religious situation in Wales. There is nothing to say that agreed syllabuses shall not encompass the whole globe, but they must at least deal with Great Britain. This represents an important development for religious education. The administration and the determination of the syllabus remains local, but the content is to become typical of Great Britain.

3. Religious education in the classroom

In Sec.8 of the Act we come to "further provisions" concerning religious education in the basic curriculum. The emphasis here is upon continuity. Religious education shall continue to be "the kind required by" the relevant sections of the 1944 Education Act, ie. Sec. 26-28 of that Act updated by special arrangements made in the 1988 Act for the situation in the Grant Maintained schools, ie. Sec. 84-86. Several aspects of that continuity have already been referred to, and others have been implied in earlier sections of the 1988 Act. For example, the 1944 legislation required religious education to be given to all pupils in maintained schools.[12] In recent years a widespread misunderstanding has arisen in which it is thought that this applies only to pupils of compulsory school age, and that those over the age of 16 were exempt. This was clearly contrary to the 1944 Act, which does not speak of pupils of a certain age but of pupils in schools. If an institution was regulated by provisions for schools as distinct from further education regulations then religious education was to be given to all the pupils in that institution, unless their parents withdrew them.

The intention of the 1988 Act is fundamentally to strengthen the provisions of the previous Act, and so it is that this particular misunderstanding is now firmly squashed. In Sec.2 when the first reference to the basic curriculum occurs, it is made clear that the requirements of the National Curriculum apply only to pupils within the compulsory school-going ages. This is only said with respect to the National

Curriculum itself and so it becomes clear that the rest of the basic curriculum (ie. religious education) applies to pupils no matter what their age is. It is clearly the responsibility of governors and heads of sixth form colleges to provide religious education as part of the basic curriculum for all their students. The only exception is made in the case of maintained special schools (2:3).

This continuity with the kind of arrangements made for religious education under the previous legislation is further emphasized by Sec.8:1 which renews the various "conscience" clauses of the older Act. Access to the maintained school system is not to be dependent upon pupils' religious practices outside school hours, the parent of any pupil may request that the pupil be withdrawn from the religious life of the school, whether in school assembly or in the basic curriculum, and parents who desire their children to receive an alternative religious education to that which the school offers in its basic curriculum may withdraw their children from the school, subject to certain conditions (Sec.9). The conditions are that it must be impossible or inconvenient to send the children to a maintained school where religious education and worship of a kind approved of by the parent are available, and that the alternative religious education must be either at the beginning or the end of the school session so as not to affect the attendance of the children too seriously.

In the past, these clauses for the provision of alternative religious worship and education were little used, mainly because the agreed syllabus and the school assembly were, on the whole, responsive to local needs. Provided this flexibility and responsibility to the local community continues, there is no reason why requests for alternative religious provision should not continue to be rather rare. Parents are represented in the arrangements for the control of religious education in various ways and it is to be expected that the needs of various groups of parents can all be catered for under the flexible arrangements of both the old and the new Acts. There is always the possibility that there will be small groups of parents whose religious views will not permit them to take part in these public procedures, nor to allow their children to receive religious education at school, but if substantial numbers of parents from significant and mainstream religious communities began to seek alternative religious worship and education, it would indicate some failure in community negotiations.

It is worth making several comments about the right of parents to withdraw their children. This is quite independent from the question about desiring an alternative form of worship and religious education. The provision of alternative religious education only applies, of course, to those who have been withdrawn, but not all those withdrawn may want an alternative. Some parents may be secularists, while others may be content that their children should receive the teachings of their religion in their own homes or out of school hours. Withdrawal has, in the past, been mainly confined to certain Christian denominations, and one suspects that often schools have not explained the educational nature of their religious policies carefully to these parents, or the parents have not always realised that their own denomination permitted a broader view of the matter.[13] We may also hope that the approach in religious education will be less instructional and more educational, since this is required by the new Act. The stronger the educational outlook and practice of religious education, and the more broadly based and balanced its curriculum, the less likely it is that parents will be afraid that their children will be subject to religious pressures of a kind inappropriate for school. At a time when certain misunderstandings of the religious significance of the new Act have been popularised by a section of the media, and some people from religions other than Christianity are feeling nervous, it is important that the true position should be clearly understood.

It must also be pointed out that the right of withdrawal belongs to the parent not to the pupil. While this is no doubt appropriate for younger children there is a point in the development of young people when they must accept responsibility for their own quest for a faith by which to live. That pupils should reach this point as soon as possible must be a sort of "attainment target" for religious education, which seeks to create a generation which accepts responsibility for its own commitments and does not simply respond to the received commitments of the older generation. It would seem more appropriate for the right of withdrawal to apply only to children up to the school leaving age. Beyond that point, either students should have the right of withdrawal for themselves or (and this seems preferable) there should be no right of withdrawal from this vital aspect of the general education of all school students. It would then be precisely because at the age of 16 their parents lose the right to have them withdrawn that these students must shoulder the responsibility of learning for themselves. Learning implies participation, always supposing that the learning is offered in a truly educational spirit. This, however, must wait for the next Education Act.

4. The content of religious education

Sec.8:3 brings us to the subject of the content of the agreed syllabuses. It has already been pointed out that while the contents of the rest of the basic curriculum are subject to the decisions of the Secretary of State the content of religious education is to be in accordance with an agreed syllabus drawn up locally.

Any new agreed syllabus "shall reflect the fact that the religious traditions in Great Britain are in the main Christian whilst taking account of the teaching and practices of the other principal religions represented in Great Britain". It is important to emphasize that, once again, the major thrust of these words is towards continuity rather than change. Education Acts have generally reflected good practice rather

9

than created it and this is no exception.

In the 19th century religious education in England and Wales was almost wholly confined to the Bible. So great was the fear of denominational proselytizing in the schools that the attention of teachers was directed away from the actual expressions of living faith and belief to the study of origins. There was, indeed, a general fear of studying religion, whether in the past or the present, and there was an interesting controversy in the 1870s and '80s as to whether the Bible should be taught without note or comment. The fear was that the teacher would not be able to avoid making some comment on contemporary religious life, although those who opposed this view argued that the teacher could hardly be said to teach the Bible at all if no comment was to be allowed.[14]

This habit of looking back to the sources of the Judaeo-Christian tradition continued more or less unabated until the early 1960s.[15] Research findings in the early 1960s showed the failure of trying to teach the Bible chronologically[16] and similar doubts were expressed about teaching the Bible with an emphasis upon Christian doctrine.[17] In the "experiential" approaches of the 1960s we find valuable efforts to make religious education more relevant and stimulating by teaching it through the experience of the children and young people, or by showing its relationship to their own experiences.[18]

The attempt to teach religion in the context of the pupils' own life and experience led to an increased emphasis upon the world today, and to the study of religious life and faith as a live option for modern people.[19] This led to a widening of the curriculum to include the major religions of the world, whilst continuing to emphasize the central importance of Christianity.[20]

These changes were naturally reflected in the agreed syllabuses. The three most famous agreed syllabuses of the 1960s were produced by the West Riding of Yorkshire, by Lancashire and by London.[21] These may be regarded as experiential Christian syllabuses. The West Riding syllabus did contain brief notes on children from Jewish homes and from Hindu, Sikh and Muslim backgrounds[22] but already by 1969 this was quite inadequate for conditions in the industrial cities of Yorkshire and in 1970 a supplement to the 1966 syllabus was issued which marked an important development in the approach which has received official sanction in the 1988 Act. Here, for the first time in a supplement to an official agreed syllabus, the approach adopted to religious education was that of studying the principal religious traditions of Britain with special reference to those found locally.[23] The emphasis upon studying religious life and faith in the contemporary world and in the communities where children live was influenced by trends in theological and religious study in the universities where the "phenomenological" approach was of growing significance.[24]

As far as the agreed syllabuses are concerned the approach which regarded religious education as consisting of the study of the principal religious traditions of Britain with an emphasis on Christianity received its definitive statement in the 1975 Birmingham Agreed Syllabus, and it is an indication of progress that religious education's recognition of the plurality of its subject matter, which was so controversial at the time, has now found a place in law. The Birmingham syllabus emphasized the educational approach to religious education, insisted on relating religion to the lives, communities and families from which students came, and required that although every pupil should study Christianity, this study should be supplemented by some familiarity with the other principal religions in Birmingham.[25] At least 70 agreed syllabuses have been produced by LEAs since Birmingham and it is important to realize that this general approach runs throughout all of them, with different emphases and perspectives.[26] It is true that very few syllabuses have been as rich in explicit content as Birmingham's, and some have tended to be more an indication of general orientations for the subject rather than a syllabus in the literal sense. This may be one of the factors leading to the emphasis in the 1988 Act upon the need for a syllabus to contain explicit religious content. The important new agreed syllabuses of recent years have not only maintained a rich content but have emphasized other points which have also found their way into the new Act. One thinks of the emphasis in the 1985 ILEA agreed syllabus on taking account of the religious background of the families of the children,[27] which is now included in the headteachers' responsibilities for the provision of religious worship.

There may still be some university departments of theology in which it is impossible to study anything which has happened in Christianity since AD 451, but that is certainly not as common as it was thirty years ago. The same has taken place in religious education in schools. Thirty years ago pupils could complete their school religious education knowing very little of Christianity as a principal religious tradition of Great Britain, and having forgotten a great deal about the prophets of the 8th century and the journeys of St. Paul. In the last fifteen years there has been a sustained attempt to teach Christianity as a living relevant faith.[28] This interest has been reflected in the publication of religious education textbooks dealing with Christianity.[29] There is no indication that this interest has declined in the last two or three years; on the contrary, the pattern is consistent. Christianity is offered as the major religious tradition of the British Isles together with studies of other principal religious traditions.[30] Needless to say, in an enterprise culture the activities of commercial publishers are a pretty reliable guide to what is actually going on in the schools.

Much fine material has been developed for the informed and responsible teaching of other major British religions including Judaism, Hinduism, the Sikh faith and perhaps most importantly Islam. This has taken place without any legal requirement, but we may now expect considerable acceleration in this area as a result of the new Act.

There has been a major teacher training effort in the past fifteen years in order to equip teachers for this kind of approach. Many religious education teachers were trained in university or college departments which emphasized the historical and exegetical study of the Bible rather than the Bible in relationship to present life and faith. Many of them studied nothing of Christainity except the development of early Christain doctrine and church history, often not going beyond the 18th or 19th centuries. These teachers have needed help in order to teach Christainity as the main living faith in Great Britain, and similar help has been necessary in order to familiarise teachers with the other principal religious traditions. It is true that not nearly enough teachers from Muslim, Sikh and Hindu backgrounds have been recruited but we may hope that as the meaning of the new Act becomes better understood this situation will gradually change.

As far as the phenomenological method is concerned, any profession contains its various schools of thought. Phenomenology has been one of the most significant of these within British religious education in recent years, but it has never been the only one. It was certainly very important for religious education and for the curriculum as a whole that the Swann Committee was informed about this approach, and found in it a viable way for religious education to operate in what is, in the main, a multicultural society.[31] Other approaches have sprung up in recent years. One thinks of the approach through religious experience led by the University of Nottingham Religious Experience Research Project[32] and the "explicit religion" approach of the Birmingham University "Religious Education in the Early Years" project.[33] Another important trend is the "human development" emphasis in the various writings of Michael Grimmitt[34] which has provided the theoretical background for the Westhill Project[35] and the recently published Roman Catholic syllabus.[36] It is probably generally agreed that the phenomenological approach has made an essential contribution to British religious education theory and practice. It cannot be ignored, and will continue to provide an essential resource, which will be corrected and/or supplemented in various ways.

It is a pity that a superficial understanding of these developments has led to a number of criticisms of contemporary religious education theory and practice which are unjustified. There are undoubtedly cases where unimaginative and perhaps poorly-trained teachers have allowed the rich and many sided phenomenological approach to degenerate into a rather meagre account of a few basic facts drawn from a range of religions wider than the pupils' experience or maturity could accommodate. This has led to sneers about "a Cook's tour of world religions", a religious "mish-mash", a religious "smorgasbord" and other jibes which have now become rather boring. Unimaginative and poorly-trained teachers have presented the Bible through a deadly battery of imports and exports into and out of the Kingdom of Solomon and a wearisome list of passages common to more than one gospel, but this has not led critics to call for teaching of the Bible to be abandoned. What we need, as always, is better teacher-training, more resources, and a more sensitive and imaginative implementation of a richer theoretical underpinning.

With this background in mind, let us now examine in detail the wording of the crucial sentence in Section 8:3.

We note that unless a new syllabus is adopted, no change at all is required in the content and practice of religious education. Since the seventy-odd agreed syllabuses of the past ten or fifteen years are, in any case, mostly consistent with the requirements of this section, it may be that many SACREs will not see fit to call for a review. However, there are cases where the agreed syllabus of an LEA will not be consistent with the requirements of this section, and these will almost always be very old syllabuses which have not been revised for thirty years or more. If the recognition offered to the new agreed syllabuses is taken as a hint by the more sluggish LEAs, then this will be all to the good.

The new wording tells us that Great Britain has a number of "religious traditions". The use of the plural here is extremely important. The British tradition is not monolithic. Not only is Christainity represented here as comprising a number of different religious traditions, but the Christian traditions as a whole are subsumed within the general category "religious traditions". We are dealing here with a social, cultural and historical phenomenon, of which the Christian expressions are, in the main, most widely represented. Moreover, the typical or general presence of the Christian traditions is only the case "in the main". It would appear, therefore, that any new agreed syllabus is not to present a sort of homogenised or uniform impression of a culturally consistent Christianity such as was often found in the agreed syllabuses of the 1920-1970 period, but in line with current practice to present the Christain faith as it is actually lived and believed by a variety of communities with a range of traditions.[37]

This is not all. Any agreed syllabus which stops short at this point has not been faithful to the Act. It will not be sufficient to present a range of Christian traditions even granting that these are not claimed to be absolutley predominant but only "in the main". The section continues "whilst taking account of the teaching and practices of the other principal religions represented in Great Britain". It seems unlikely that there is any significant difference between "shall reflect" and "taking account of", so it seems reasonable to conclude that the significance and weight of the requirement lies in both its major elements. This does not necessarily mean, of course, that any actual syllabus should be equally weighted between the mainly Christian traditions and the other principal religions. Sometimes more significance would be given to Christianity; sometimes more significance would be given to the other religious traditions. It will depend upon a number of factors, one of which will certainly be the composition of the area. The significant thing to note is, however, that it will no longer be possible for parts of the country which are predominantly Christian, or where there are no significant groups of religious adherence other than Christian, to claim that therefore the local agreed syllabus should exclude the other principal religions. The locus of study is not to be the local county but Great Britain. Islam may not be a particularly significant religion in every rural part of East Anglia or the West country, but on any reckoning it is a principal religion represented in Great Britain. [38] This does not mean that the older, unrevised agreed syllabuses which concentrate on the Bible and Christianity are illegal. There is no legal requirement for revision, and it is perfectly possible that they might go on unrevised for decades. As soon, however, as a review of the old agreed syllabus is initiatied and a new syllabus is prepared, the Christian monopoly must be broken. This is the unmistakable implication of the 1988 Education Reform Act.

It is important to notice that some details are offered about how agreed syllabuses are to take account of the other principal religions in Great Britain. They are to take account of "the teaching and practices" of them. The teaching includes the doctrine and other aspects of the beliefs of the religion.

For the first time, therefore, the basic curriculum of children and young people in our schools will not be meeting the legal standards unless they are taught the teaching of the principal non-Christian religions in Great Britain. This will naturally take place in a way appropriate to the age, family background and aptitude of the pupils, as it always has done, and this is doubtless what is meant by saying that these matters are to be taken into account. Although, as was noted, there can hardly be a difference between reflecting and taking account of, it is perhaps significant that both these expressions imply a certain distance. The wording does not tell us that the agreed syllabuses shall contain the teaching of Christianity and other religions or that Christian and other religions shall be taught. Rather, whatever syllabus is drawn up shall reflect and take account of these realities. It is clear that this leaves a wide margin of educational discretion and will prove flexible enough to be adaptable to the needs of most situations in England and Wales. Great Britain is, of course, larger than England and Wales, and it is interesting to note that it would be appropriate for agreed syllabuses to reflect Christian and non-Christian religions in both Scotland and Northern Ireland, in so far as these are deemed to be relevant to the educational needs of children in England and Wales. Once again, a wide range of selection and a flexible approach is called for.

Chapter 2

THE RELIGIOUS LIFE OF THE SCHOOL AS A WHOLE

1. Collective Worship

Sections 6 and 7 of the Act deal with school worship. In these Sections school worship is described either as "collective worship" or simply as "worship". In Section 1, 9 and 11 the expression "religious worship" is used. In Section 12 the Act describes "Christian collective worship" but this refers to a part only of the religious worship or collective worship which is to take place in the school. The Act is clear and consistent in refusing to describe school worship as being Christian. Christian worship is part of religious worship, and when we are discussing the whole school, particularly as focussed in the act of worship, it is important that we remember this distinction. To put it baldly, Christian collective worship is optional for schools but religious collective worship is compulsory.

Unless their parents withdraw them wholly or partly from it, "all pupils in attendance at a maintained school shall on each school day take part in an act of collective worship"(6:1). Special schools are exempt from this requirement. There may be one act of worship for the entire school or pupils may take part in acts of worship in their age groups or other school groups. Headteachers and school governors are responsible for these arrangements and are required to consult with each other. The school worship shall normally take place on the school premises.

The effect of this section is to clarify responsibility for the conduct of school worship, and at the same time, to offer a more flexible pattern. Under the 1944 Act the collective act of worship had to take place at the beginning of each school day, and had to be a single act of worship on the part of all the pupils in attendance unless there was no room or hall in the school suitable for such a large gathering. Under the new arrangements the assembly may take place at any time during the day and may or may not consist of the entire school. Pupils may gain access to the required daily worship through their form, year group, pastoral group, house or through any other kind of structure, provided it is a group which has a life of its own in the school and is not created specifically for the purpose of the act of worship. One could not, for example, in a school where there was a minority of Muslim pupils treat those pupils as a school group and arrange a daily act of Islamic worship especially for them, unless those Muslim pupils were already meeting as a school group in some other regular function of school life.

Here again, we see that the 1988 Act confirms what has become widespread practice in the schools. It has been very common for schools to have their assembly after morning registration or after the first period, or after the morning break. Similarly, many secondary schools have been regularly providing not one but many acts of school worship. There are large comprehensive schools where the number of such regular assemblies has been more than twenty each week. Schools have been guided in this not merely by the nature of their premises but by educational considerations. This is as it should be, and Section 6 of the new Act recognises it. The educational context of all this is recognised in the requirement that the groups into which the school breaks down for purposes of worship shall be groups which function regularly in the life of the school. The intention is not to create an atmosphere of confessional devotion, with pupils being divided into groups based on their various religious commitments, but to create something which is appropriate for a maintained school.

2. Wholly or Mainly of a Broadly Christian Character

So far, the Act has described what we might call the normal or basic requirment for school worship. In Section 7 we move on to what are described as "special provisions". Here we find something which is radically new. Just as the 1944 Act said nothing positive about the content of classroom religious education, except that it had to be in accordance with an agreed syllabus, so it said nothing positive about the content of the collective act of worship. We were told what it should not be, but not what it should be: school worship shall not "be distinctive of any particular religious denomination" (1944 Education Act Section 26). In other words, school worship could not be conducted regularly in accordance with the Book of Common Prayer, nor in accordance with the Quaker custom. Nothing positive was said about what school worship should be like, and the most authoritative source of guidance has traditionally been the agreed syllabuses, which have often included a section on this.

The new wording is as follows. The collective worship "shall be wholly or mainly of a broadly Christian character" (7:1). The following sub-section (7:2) offers guidance on what is meant by "broadly" and the section after that clarifies the expression "wholly or mainly". "...collective worship is of a broadly Christian character if it reflects the broad traditions of Christian belief without being distinctive of any particular Christian denomination"(7:2). "Every act of collective worship... need not (be wholly or mainly of a broadly Christian character) provided that, taking any school term as a whole, most such acts which take place in the school do comply..."(7:3).

It is, perhaps, natural that when new legislation comes into force it is seen as imposing restrictions rather than as granting freedoms. In interpreting these clauses we must pay equal attention to both what is required and what is not required. Let us first notice that insofar as acts of collective worship are to be Christian at all, they are to be "wholly or mainly" so. This presents us with the first alternative inviting freedom. There is no requirement here that any act of school collective worship should be wholly Christian. "Wholly" and "mainly" are offered as alternatives.

A school may choose to go "wholly" or to go "mainly" if it decides to accept a pattern of Christian worship. This is the option which is, in the first place, available to the head and the governors of every county school.

Mainly what? "...mainly... broadly Christian..." The wording does not say bluntly "mainly Christian" but offers a circumlocution which is so general as to demand definition in the next sub-section. We may observe, however, that the wording selected is "broadly" Christian, not "specifically" or "typically" or "uniquely" Christian. The worship could not possibly be typical of Christian worship, since it cannot be "distinctive of any particular Christian denomination". Needless to say, nearly all of the actual collective worship which takes place within Christianity occurs within Christian denominations, which is why collective worship in schools cannot be actually or typically or concretely Christian in this specific way. That is another aspect of the importance attached to the educational context of these acts of collective school worship. They are thus precisely not church worship but school worship. The persons responsible for them are not priests or ministers (although these may take part by invitation) but headteachers and governors of schools.

Broadly what? "Mainly of a broadly Christian character". Once more we notice the careful choice of words. We are not told that school worship shall conform to Christian liturgy, nor that it shall simply be "Christian". It is, rather, to be of a "broadly Christian character". The meaning of this is elaborated in the following sentence. "...collective worship is of a broadly Christian character if it reflects the broad traditions of Christian belief without being distinctive of any particular Christian denomination". The character of collective worship is to be found not in a presentation or an application or a rendition but in a reflection.

A reflection of what? These acts of collective worship (if any take place: see below) are to reflect "the broad traditions of Christian belief". We notice here, as in the case of the agreed syllabuses, that the plurality of the Christian faith is fully recognised. There is not one tradition of Christianity but many. If we are asked what are the main traditions of Christianity, we might be inclined to reply that there are three: Protestantism, Catholicism and Orthodoxy. These, however, are probably to be regarded as denominational for the purposes of the Act and so we must be looking for something other than these, or broader than these. So it is that we are directed not towards the actual traditions or the historical traditions but the "broad traditions".

Broad traditions of what? It is significant that the Act does not speak of the broad traditions of Christian worship, natural though that form of wording must have seemed, but of the "broad traditions of Christian belief". Christian belief, therefore, is to be regarded as plural, as traditional, and as broad. It is this which is to impress a "Christian character" upon school worship.

We have already seen that the governors or head of a school could, in the first instance, opt for "mainly" rather than "wholly" and we have now seen what that "mainly" must reflect. The next Section (7:3) tells us that it is sufficient if in any school term most of the acts of collective worship are mainly (not wholly) of this character. Again we repeat the point that none of them need to be wholly of this broadly Christian character, but the majority of them must be at least mainly so.

The effect of this is to produce a number of combinations. It would be in keeping with the spirit of the Act and consistent with its wording if a school were to decide that during any one week three days would be devoted to acts which would be mainly of a broadly Christian character while the other two would be something else. At this point it is important for us to realise that the Act does not identify collective worship with Christian worship. The requirement for religious worship insists that it shall take place on each day, but the requirement for Christian collective worship is such that it need take place on no more than most days. This is consistent with the requirement for the agreed syllabuses: there are a number of religious traditions in Britain and of these Christianity is the most significant. Similarly, there are a number of ways of worshipping and of these the various Christian ways, or the ways which reflect the broad traditions of Christian belief are the most significant. Christian worship is part of a whole.

So, let us suppose that on Monday, Wednesday and Friday we have collective worship which is mainly of a broadly Christian character. It would be perfectly in order for those acts of collective worship to include materials which were not of a Christian character at all. Moreover, we must take account of the fact that the materials which do reflect the Christian traditions can be extremely various. For example, whatever the broad traditions of Christian belief may contain, they certainly contain belief in God. Any religious material which deals with God may be said to reflect this Christian tradition of belief. Inasmuch as Islam, Christianity and Judaism all represent the Abrahamic tradition they may be said to reflect one another. It is important to remember that religious traditions are not discrete and self-enclosed but mutually mingle and influence each other. Many of the stories of the saints, for example, are found in various religions, attributed to different saints. The Jewish doctrine of angels which came into the New Testament was influenced by Zoroastrianism (the modern Parsis) and Zoroastrianism may thus be said to reflect Christian belief in this respect, or the reverse. Wilfred Cantwell Smith has shown in his many writings the ways in which doctrines and traditions have passed from one religious tradition into another and back again.[39] It would take a panel of theologians to determine the limits of this reflection of the broad traditions of Christian belief, and they would almost certainly not agree. It is difficult to see the legal

18

profession in Britain having much stomach for this kind of thing, and the most natural way forward is for the schools to interpret the requirement in the general spirit of freedom and tolerance, bearing in mind the educational context of their work and the varied backgrounds of the pupils and the teachers. This is, indeed, exactly what the next section of the Act suggests.

3. Educationally Appropriate Worship

Whether the acts of collective worship are wholly or mainly of a broadly Christian character or not, and whether they occupy all or only the majority of the days of each term, they are to be appropriate for the pupils concerned (7:4).

This is something else completely new. The 1944 Act said nothing about school worship being appropriate to the pupils. It is possible to trace the sections in the various agreed syllabuses over the decades which deal with school worship, and to find frequent appeals to those responsible for school worship that they should create occasions which were appropriate for children. The vast literature on this subject which appeared after the Second World War (although one could trace it back much earlier) had this problem as its principal burden.[40] Again and again it has been emphasised that one cannot simply take hymns and prayers and Bible readings such as might be used in churches or with adults and create a kind of "service" for schools. This breadth of practice and this flexibility of approach, as demanded by the many kinds of pupils and schools, is suggested in the clause which refers to "the ways in which those traditions are reflected in any such act of collective worship" (7:4(c)). One must consider first the kind of "reflection" and then the way of making this reflection appropriate to the pupils. The implication is that there are many reflections and many ways.

In determining how school worship shall become appropriate to its context, a number of "relevant circumstances" are suggested in 7:5. These are "any circumstances relating to the family backgrounds of the pupils concerned which are relevant to determining the character of the collective worship which is appropriate in their case" together with "their ages and aptitudes". We see then that the word "character" occurs in two ways in this description of the collective acts of school worship. There is a character which reflects the family backgrounds of the pupils together with their ages and aptitudes, i.e. a character which we can describe as "appropriate". Secondly, there is that feature of some school acts of worship by virtue of which they reflect a broadly Christian character. The latter is optional; the former is not. The pupils take priority over all other considerations. One can dispense with the Christian character but one cannot dispense with the character of that which is appropriate for the pupils. Here we must applaud those who framed the new Education Act. The order of priorities is surely correct. Acts of school worship may only reflect a broadly Christian character if that is considered to be appropriate for the pupils concerned. If a Christian character would not be appropriate, then some other and more appropriate kind of religious worship must be provided.

In the case of many pupils their family backgrounds will not represent any religious tradition at all. They will come from homes where there is no overt attachment to any place of worship and where religious beliefs and values are at best implicit. What kind of religious worship would be appropriate for these pupils?

It must be remembered that the appropriateness is, of course, an educational appropriateness. This is, after all, an Education Act, not an Act determining the rights and powers of religious bodies. It would be wrong for an enthusiastic religious believer who happened to be a headteacher to conclude that collective worship of a positively Christian character was appropriate precisely because his or her pupils had no family background whatever relevant to Christianity. The appropriateness in this case would be of an evangelical kind, and this is clearly not what is envisaged in the Act. It is, of course, open to the parents of such children to withdraw them, but here one is dealing with the more self-conscious, more deliberate Humanist or Secularist parent rather than with the general mass of secularised modern British families. It would be appropriate in such cases that there should be a very sympathetic interpretation of the requirement about reflecting a broadly Christian character, and that this reflection should be such as to come within the interests and comprehension of these secularised pupils.

One must, in such cases, think of educating pupils into various possibilities of worship, of creating a "threshold of worship"[41], of thinking about the basic elements or intentions in religion which are of a worshipful kind and constructing a sort of ladder of words and music which reaches down to where the pupils are, and so on. We must, in other words, be sensitive and realistic as teachers, whilst giving full weight to the importance of the spiritual quest in the life and experience of all children.

What the new Act clearly rules out altogether, and this is reinforcing the previous Act, is the kind of school assembly which had itself become merely secular and administrative. There are too many schools, particularly at the secondary level, where assembly has lost all contact with worship. School assemblies are used for the reading of notices and for moralising speeches intended to maintain school "tone". The new Act says that this is not enough. Collective worship is to be taken up into the educational programme of the school; it is to be part of the school curriculum.[42] It is to make a definite contribution to the pupils' search for a faith by which to live, it is to contribute to the spiritual development of the pupil, of the school as a whole and of the society. This is to take place through worship which will generally be of a Christian character but must always be modified so as to be appropriate to the real-life needs of children and young people.

If interpreted sensibly and not dogmatically, educationally and not evangelistically, spiritually but not confessionally and always consistently with dialogue, the results will be a renewal of a central part of the British school experience. If, however, the Act is interpreted in a sectarian manner, whether that be thought of denominationally or whether Christianity as a whole is seen as a sect, the result will be a deterioration of community relations, and the imposition upon pupils of inappropriate forms of religious life which will serve but to deepen any present alienation from the spiritual quest.

In the above discussion we have been exploring the freedom which the schools are permitted under the new legislation. What if even this is not enough in some situations? What will happen in those schools where, even when they have chosen the "mainly" and rejected the "wholly" alternative, and have opted for this only on three days of the week, and have interpreted the Christian character in the broad non-sectarian way which we have suggested, so that there is dialogue and exchange between different ways of worship and different religious traditions, there remains a problem?

There will be many such schools. They will be schools in which pupils, far from coming from mainly secular backgrounds will come from families rich in religious traditions which are not Christian. It would be wise for the governing bodies and heads of such schools to explore to the full the freedom offered in Sections 6 and 7 of the Act before going any further, and it would be premature to conclude on the basis of press reports and an over-enthusiastic interpretation from some Christian groups that the requirements for collective worship will not work in a multi-faith school. Nevertheless, there will certainly be some schools, and perhaps many, where this will be the case. These will be the many hundreds of schools with significant minorities or majorities of pupils from mainly Hindu, Muslim, Sikh and other religious backgrounds which are not Christian. Section 7:6 anticipates this situation.

4. The Multi-Faith School

In the situation described in the previous paragraph the headteacher and/or the governing body may make application to the local Standing Advisory Council for Religious Education (SACRE) to be exempt from the requirement that the majority of school assemblies should be mainly of a broadly Christian character. Such an application may be made on behalf of the entire school, in which case such a school would no longer be required to have any assemblies at all which reflected the broad traditions of Christian belief, or the application may be made on behalf of certain pupils, whether or not these pupils happen to form groups which function otherwise in the school life. The decision regarding such an application is to be made by the SACRE, and is called a "determination". Let us distinguish between SACRE-determined (SACRE-d) and Section-7-determined (Section-d). In the section which deals with the powers of SACRE (Section 12) we learn that the SACRE-d assemblies are less permanent than the Section-d ones, since the determination given by SACRE only holds good for five years. Application may be made for the renewal of the determination, but if no application is made, the SACRE-d assembly would lapse and it would so to speak fall back into the Section-d assembly situation. We see then that the Section-d assembly is the norm, the level to which by passage of time assembly tends to resettle, but there is clear provision for maintaining a SACRE-d assembly indefinitely by repeated determinations, and no doubt this situation will become commonplace. Nothing is said about the number of such SACRE-d assemblies which may take place in any school. Application can be made on behalf of pupils of any description, and it is perfectly possible that there will be several such SACRE-d assemblies in a school. It would be perfectly in order for a SACRE-d assembly to comprise the majority of the school and for the Section-d gathering to take place in a classroom for only a handful.

There are, however, restrictions placed upon the content of SACRE-d assemblies. In the first place, the SACRE does not have the power to determine that a school or a group of pupils within a school will not have to take part in an act of collective worship each day. The SACRE can approve of a school not holding Christian collective worship, but it cannot approve of a school not having worship at all. In this sense, as we have already seen, Christian collective worship is optional, but worship as such is not optional. Parents who do not want their children to worship at all in school must make application for them to be withdrawn. Presumably, a parent could request that a pupil be withdrawn from a SACRE-d assembly just as from a Section-d assembly. But what is to be the character of these SACRE-d acts of worship? They "shall not be distinctive of any particular Christian or other religious denomination (but this shall not be taken as preventing that worship from being distinctive of any particular faith)" (7:6(b)).

We see that it would not be possible for a SACRE to grant permission to hold an Anglican act of worship. Similarly, there could not be a SACRE-d assembly for Catholic pupils, or for Quakers, or for Jehovah's Witnesses. By the same token, no SACRE-d assembly could be distinctive of any denomination of another religion. It would be permissible, however, for a SACRE-d assembly to be distinctive of a particular faith. The Act does not say that a SACRE-d assembly *must* be distinctive of a faith, merely that it *may* be. If a SACRE-d assembly is not *required* to be distinctive of a faith, and is not *permitted* to be distinctive of a denomination within a faith, it is not easy to see what a SACRE-d act of worship would consist of, but this does not matter. It simply illustrates the wide freedom and the lack of definition which is characteristic of these provisions for school worship in general.

The wording of this clause distinguishes religious denominations from faiths. A "faith" is presumably the same as one of the "religious traditions" mentioned in connection with the new agreed syllabuses, but it is important to observe that a SACRE-d act of worship need not be distinctive of one of the *principal* religious traditions in Great Britain. The latter are reserved for classroom study, but in a SACRE-d assembly it is sufficient that the group of pupils constitute a faith, regardless of how small that faith may be. The group must, however, show that it is indeed an independent faith, and not a denomination within a larger faith. We must hope that SACREs will have well-informed theologians to advise them in cases of doubt.

In general, the provisions for both Section-d and SACRE-d types of worship present schools with a wide range of possibilities. If interpreted with sensitivity, these should lead to a heightened profile for the religious life of the school. Commitment should come to be more important, and spiritualities should thus be taken more seriously. In schools where pupils come from several religious traditions, one possible outcome might be for the acts of worship on (say) Monday, Wednesday and Friday to be "wholly or mainly of a broadly Christian character" and for SACRE-d acts of worship distinctive of other faiths to take place at the same time. On a Tuesday and Thursday, when it is not required that the act of worship should reflect Christian belief at all, it would be possible to have acts of worship involving mutual understanding, celebration and exploration, in which the communities of faith would come to appreciate each other more fully. Some Christians might claim that acts of worship of this kind, particularly when closely related in this way to the age, aptitude and family background of pupils, would reflect very well certain broad traditions of Christian belief, but in that case there would be no reason why they should not take place every day, by mutual agreement within the school.

On the other hand, if some Christians were to take an aggressive stance, insisting that all Section-d acts of collective worship in the school should reflect the broad traditions of Christian belief (although this is not required by the Act) and should moreover demand that these broad traditions are not merely reflected but are actually insisted upon and presented in a vivid way (thus not only going far beyond the requirements of the Act but possibly infringing the Act), it is likely that SACREs will be called upon to authorise many more acts of worship and in such situations relationships between religious communities are likely to become strained and competitive. This could well overflow into the classroom, and schools could all too easily become divided along religious lines. Acts of school worship, whether Section-d or SACRE-d, should be joyful celebrations of value and meaning, not defensive reassertions of threatened identity. Provided that all religious groups remember that the Act clearly subordinates religious to educational considerations and seeks to make the spirituality of religious groups available for educational communities, this danger will be avoided. It is to be feared that not all religious groups will have the humility or the restraint to accept this understanding of their role. A heavy burden of responsibility rests upon SACREs, governing bodies, headteachers and the staff of religious education departments to educate the religious communities in their locality to their new responsibilities under the 1988 Education Reform Act.

Chapter 3

THE ADMINISTRATION OF RELIGIOUS EDUCATION

Under the 1944 Act local education authorities were responsible for the adoption of an agreed syllabus. In order to do this, it was necessary to convene a conference especially for the purpose. Schedule 5 of the 1944 Act described how this was to be done. When the resulting syllabus was finally adopted, the work of the conference would cease and it would be disbanded, never to meet again unless a review of the syllabus was necessary. A provision was made for local education authorities to appoint Standing Advisory Councils for Religious Education, but they were not required to do so, and only a handful of the LEAs in England and Wales have availed themselves of this possibility. This has left a serious gap in the administrative provision for religious education. There was no way whereby the parties who had agreed in creating the religious education for their area could check on progress, compare notes or make suggestions. For its part, the LEA could certainly appoint a religious education adviser, and many did so, but the adviser would lack the support of any properly convened and recognised body.

The new arrangements rectify this omission, and are amongst the most important provisions for religious education in the present Act. SACREs are now mandatory. Their function is to give advice on the religious worship and the religious education carried out in the schools of the LEAs. Councils are especially authorised to give advice on "methods of teaching, the choice of materials and the provision of training for teachers".

A SACRE is to be composed of four representative groups and this structure is exactly modelled upon that of the conferences which are to adopt the agreed syllabuses. The first representative group is to consist of "Christian and other religious denominations" and that form of words is now used for this group in the SACRE and in the agreed syllabus conference. It is a small but significant change. Previously, in the agreed syllabus conferences, this group was known as the "other denominations" committee, and there was occasional discussion about whether it was permissible to have representatives of religions other than Christianity on it. It could be argued that because the next committee was representative of the Church of England, the reference to "other denominations" clearly meant "other Christian denominations". In spite of this ambiguity agreed syllabus conferences for approximately twenty years have been including representatives of several faiths in the "other denominations" committee.[43]

This ambiguity is now removed. The non-Christian religious denominations are present on exactly the same footing as the Christian denominations, namely if "in

25

the opinion of the authority" they "appropriately reflect the principal religious traditions in the area" (11:4(a)). So it is that the emphasis upon pluralism and the opening of the curriculum to world religions which we saw in the provisions for the content of the agreed syllabuses, is consistently carried through to the administration of the subject.

The other groups are to represent the Church of England (except in Wales), teachers' associations, and the LEA itself. As well as these four (or in Wales three) representative groups, the SACRE may contain one representative of the governing bodies of grant maintained schools where the LEA agreed syllabus is in use, and co-opted members.

Each SACRE is free to arrange its own rules for the conduct of business, except that voting must take place in groups i.e. each representative group having one vote. It is to be hoped, however, that an atmosphere of mutual trust and informality will be established in SACREs from the first, and that the taking of a formal vote will be a very rare occasion. SACREs should conduct most of their business by indications of opinion around the table, member by member.

The SACRE has a number of significant powers. In the first place, it can require a review of the LEA agreed syllabus. In coming to the decision, the LEA group on SACRE does not itself have a vote. The decision is thus entirely a matter for the religious representatives and the teachers' associations. When an LEA receives notice of such a decision, it is required to convene a Conference in order to carry out the review. In view of the fact that the representative groups are the same, it would seem sensible to ask the SACRE to re-convene as an agreed syllabus conference, but this decision would be within the discretion of the LEA. It would be open to them to ask the represented groups to nominate a different set of persons to constitute the committees of the agreed syllabus conference.

The SACRE is required to publish a report each year on its activities. The report has to describe the advice which the SACRE has given to its LEA during the year. If this was offered gratuitously, i.e. without the SACRE being asked by the LEA for its advice, then the SACRE has to indicate why it was offered in the first place.

One of the most important powers of SACRE has to do with collective worship in schools. In Chapter 2 (4) above we discussed the situation which a headteacher or a governing body might find itself in when it was not appropriate to hold acts of worship which were wholly or mainly of a broadly Christian character. It is the SACRE which has the power to release the school from the obligation to hold these school assemblies. In an important sense therefore SACRE is the guardian of the rights of the religious minorities, or majorities as the case may be, and the nurturer of the multi-faith school. It would also be the responsibility of the SACRE to ensure that governing bodies and headteachers are aware of the great freedom and flexibility offered to them by the Act on school worship, and to see that these possibilities have been fully explored before approaching SACRE for a release. In the vast majority of schools, it may be best if SACRE is not called upon, but that the requirement for an act of collective worship which will be of a broadly Christian character is interpreted in a broadly Christian manner, i.e. so as not to create a sense of exclusion and resentment on the part of others.

The Act provides a number of other instructions about the details of SACRE administration, mainly to do with the procedures for granting exemption from Christian collective worship, but we need not go into these at this point, since our purpose is to describe the implications of the Act for religious education and is not intended to be a detailed guide for administrators.

CONCLUSION

As we have seen, the major contributions which the new Act makes to religion in the life of the school, lie in the areas of curriculum and school worship, where there is a more specific requirement as to content, and in the administration of the subject, where the powers and responsibilities of both local and national government are considerably strengthed. As far as the administrative strengthening goes, this can bring nothing but good, provided that those repsonsible are able to secure the resources and the trained teachers actually to deliver the subject in the school effectively. As far as the more specific provisions for education and worship are concerned, there must remain a question about the appropriateness of this legislation. The success of religious education for more than a century depended, to some extent, on a minimal legal definition which made it possible for new ideas to appear and for the natural process of professional and community development to take place. It is difficult to resist the view that legislation on matters of religious faith (and surely worship must spring from faith) is a curious and delicate area for parliament to get involved in, and it will be interesting to see whether the judgement of history will attribute greater wisdom to Butler or to Baker. This pamphlet, however, is not intended to discuss what kind of legislation would be appropriate for this area nor to philosophise about the nature of religious education, but to offer an explanation and interpretation of what the Act actually says. Here the 1988 Act is similar to its great predecessor in 1944, in that the prevailing practice of religious education is confirmed and the educational context of what is done is, on the whole, strengthened.

Although we emphasise the continuity, we must not underestimate the stimulus which this new legislation can and should provide. LEAs which have not considered their religious education policies for many years will be encouraged to do so, and we must hope that this will lead to a new wave of religious education curriculum development. Continuity implies evolution, not stagnation, and there may well be a need for new agreed syllabus work to be done even in LEAs where there has been renewal during the 1970s and '80s. We cannot assume that a syllabus which led the way ten years ago will be the best available for tomorrow. We may also hope that many young people from Muslim, Jewish, Hindu and other religious backgrounds will be encouraged by the new Act to join with Christians in seeking professional training as religious education teachers. The schools and the public will be looking to government, both national and local, to encourage the curriculum research, the new initiatives in teacher education and the other resource implications of the 1988 Act.

NOTES

1.　　All the references to the Act are from Part 1 *Schools* Chapter One *The Curriculum*.

2.　　Dennis J Bates, *The Nature and Place of Religion in English State Education c1900-c1944*, University of Lancaster, unpublished Ph.D. thesis, 1976, p.36. Bates goes on to discuss the rise in the late nineteenth and early twentieth centuries of the idea of religious education as formation of the entire personality as opposed to an inert and external acquisition of facts through instruction. This development occurred under the influence of philosphical idealism which retained its importance in British education until the Second World War or shortly afterwards.

3.　　*Manchester Diocesan Conference: Memorandum on religious education*, 1923. p.2.

4.　　ibid.

5.　　Basil A. Yeaxlee, *The Approach to Religious Education in Sunday School and Day School*, London, 1931, p.107. Basil A. Yeaxlee was then Principal of Westhill College in Birmingham and in 1934 became the founder editor of the journal *Religion in Education* (since 1978 the *British Journal of Religious Education*).

6.　　ibid.

7.　　ibid.

8.　　T.E. Jessop, *Evangelism and Education: the presentation of religion to adults*, London, 1947, p.43.

9.　　F.H. Hilliard, et al. *Christianity in Education* (The Hibbert Lectures, 1965) London, Allen & Unwin, 1966. Lecture 2 "Christianity in the County Schools", pp.29-49.

10.　　Edwin Cox, "Educational religious education", now in John M. Hull (Ed.) *New Directions in Religious Education*, Falmer Press, 1983, pp.53-59.

11.   For an example of the use of the concept of "balance" in religious education see British Humanist Association *Objective, Fair and Balanced; A New Law for Religious Education*, London, 1977. For further examples of the growth of an educational understanding of the role of religion in maintained schools see: Edwin Cox *Changing Aims in Religious Education*, Routledge and Kegan Paul, 1966. Ninian Smart and Donald Horder (Eds.) *New Movements in Religious Education*, Temple Smith, 1975.
Jean Holm *Teaching Religion in School*, Oxford University Press, 1977.
John M. Hull *Studies in Religion and Education*, Falmer Press, 1984, especially chs. 3 and 4.
For the concept of religious education contributing to the humanisation of schools, society and pupils see mostly recently Michael H. Grimmitt *Religious Education and Human Development*, McCrimmon Publishing Co., 1987.

12.   "Religious instruction shall be given in every county school and in every voluntary school". 1944 Education Act Section 25:2.

13.   Roger Homan "Teaching the Children of Jehovah's Witnesses". *BJRE*, 10 (Summer 1988), pp.154-159.

14.   For a brief history on the main stages through which the teaching of the Bible has passed in British religious education see John M. Hull *The Bible in the Secular Classroom: An approach through the Experience of Loss*, North of England Institute for Christian Education, Durham, 1986, and especially page 12 for the question of teaching the Bible 'without note or comment'.

15.   For discussion of the content of the agreed syllabuses before 1960 see John M Hull "Agreed Syllabuses, Past, Present and Future" in *Studies*, op. cit., pp.73-93.

16.   Harold Loukes, *New Ground in Christian Education*, SCM Press, 1965, Colin Alves, *Religious Education and the Secondary School*, SCM Press, 1968.

17.   Ronald Goldman, *Religious Thinking from Childhood to Adolescence*, Routledge and Kegan Paul, 1964.

18.   Ronald Goldman, *Readiness for Religion*, Routledge and Kegan Paul, 1965. And for critical surveys see John M. Hull in *Studies*, op. cit. chap. 11, 12, 13.

19.	Two examples illustrating this emphasis and taken from opposite ends of the school-age spectrum might be Violet Madge, *Children in Search of Meaning*, SCM Press, 1965 and Edwin Cox, *Sixth Form Religion*, SCM Press, 1967.

20.	For a brief history of the study of world religions in schools see Dennis J. Bates, op.cit., pp.281-290.

21.	*Suggestions for Religious Education, West Riding Agreed Syllabus*, 1966, Lancashire Education Committee *Religion and Life: Agreed Syllabus* 1968, *Learning for Life,*
The Agreed Syllabus of Religious Education of the Inner London Education Authority, 1968.

22.	*Suggestions for Religious Education*, op.cit., pp.104f.

23.	*Guide to Religious Education n a Multi-Faith Communtiy*, Bradford supplement to the 1966 West Riding Agreed Syllabus. n.d. (1970)

24.	Ninian Smart, *Secular Education and the Logic of Religion*, Faber, 1968 was a harbinger of this emphasis which was expressed in the influential Schools Council Working Paper 36 *Religious Education in Secondary Schools*, Evans/Methuen, 1971.

For more recent studies of the phenomenological approach to the teaching of religion in school see: Stephen J. Reno "Distance in the Study of Religion", *BJRE* 1 (Spring 1979), pp.108-110.
Kenneth Surin "Can the Experiential and the Phenomenological Approaches be Reconciled?" *BJRE* 2 (Spring 1980), pp.99-103.
Ian L. Higgins "The Phenomenological Approach to the Teaching of Christianity in the Secondary School in Year 10" *BJRE* 3 (Spring 1981), pp.100-101.
Bent Smidt Hansen "Phenomenology of Religion: A Bridge betweeen the Scholarly Study of Religion and Religious Education" *BJRE* 6 (Autumn 1983), pp.14-19.

25.	City of Birmingham District Council Education Committee *Agreed Syllabus of Religious Instruction*, 1975, see also the 1977 Handbook and the 1982 supplement to the Handbook.

26.	Roger B. Howarth, *Agreed Syllabuses of Religious Education 1975-1982; educational, religious and social factors which have influenced their development*, University of Birmingham, unpublished M.Ed. dissertation, 1983.

27.   *Religious Education for our Children. The Agreed Syllabus of the Inner London Education Authority*, 1985.

28.   See for example the symposium on *Christianity* in *Learning for Living* 13 (March 1974).

Roy Niblett "Christian Education: Authority and Communication", *BJRE* 4 (Spring 1982), pp.76-79.

Harry Undy "Christianity as a World Religion", *BJRE* 4 (Spring 1982), pp.80-87.

Trevor and Margaret Cooling "Christian Doctrine in Religious Education", *BJRE* 9 (Summer 1987), pp.152-159.

Jeff Astley "Theology and Curriculum Selection", *BJRE* 10 (Spring 1988) pp.86-91.

29.   A few examples only can be given here.

Rankin, John et al. *The Chichester Project* (Series on Christianity), Lutterworth Education 1982.

Jan Thompson *Christian Belief and Practice*, Edward Arnold Ltd., 1983.

Alan Brown *The Christian World* (Religions of the World Series), Macdonald Educational, 1984.

John E. Greer, and E.P. McElhinney, *Irish Christianity: Five Units for Secondary Pupils*, Dublin, Gill and Macmillan, 1985.

Sarah Thorley *Christianity in Words and Pictures*, RMEP, 1985.

V. Cross and P. Taylor *Christian Worship* (Holt World Religions Series), Holt, Rinehart and Winston, 1986.

Stephen W. Harrison and David Shepherd *A Christian Family in Britain*, RMEP, 1986.

D. Self, *Stories from the Christian World*, Macdonald, 1986.

Chignell. M.A. *Framework: Christianity and Life*, Edward Arnold, 1987.

M. Keene, *The Development of Christianity* (Investigations in Religion Series), Blackwell, 1987.

Garth Read et al. *Christianity - Teachers' Manual* plus *Christianity* Books 1 to 4 (The Westhill Project) Mary Glasgow Publications, 1987.

Kevin O'Donnell, *Christianity: An Approach for GCSE*, Edward Arnold, 1987.

James P. Taylor, *The Christian Story*, Edward Arnold, 1988.

Jan Thompson, *The Many Paths of Christianity*, Edward Arnold, 1988.

30.   See for example the *Looking at World Religions Series*, Longman, 1987.
Living Festivals Series, RMEP, 1987.
Discovering Religions Series, Heinemann 1987,
World Religions Series, Bell and Hyman 1986, and many others.

31.	*Education for All*, (The Swann Report) H.M.S.O. 1985, especially ch. 8 on religious education.

32.	David Hay et al. *New Methods in Religious Education: An Experiential Approach* (The Religious Experience and Education Project), Oliver and Boyd/Longman, 1989 (in press).

33.	Publications forthcoming.

34.	In addition to the work cited, see his "World Religions and Personal Development" in Robert Jackson (ed.) *Approaching World Religions*, John Murray, 1982, pp.136-149 and *Religious Education and Humanisation*, Australian Association for Religious Education, 1983.

35.	Garth Read et al. *How Can I Teach RE?* (The Westhill Project), Mary Glasgow Publications, 1987.

36.	Richard Lohan and Mary McClure, *Weaving the Web: a modular programme of Religious Education for Archdiocesan Secondary Schools*, Collins Liturgical, 1988, *Teacher's Book*, p.9.

37.	It is estimated that Christianity includes 150 principal ecclesiastical traditions and at least 20,800 distinct denominations. See David B. Barrett (ed) *World Christian Encyclopedia*, OUP, 1982.

38.	Moreover these are becoming principal religions of Great Britain. There are twice as many Muslims as Methodists in Great Britain, and there are more Sikhs than all the Quakers, Salvation Army and Lutherans put together. See Peter Brierley (ed) *UK Christian Handbook 1989/90 Edition*, MARC Europe, 1988, pp.166-176.

39.	Wilfred Cantwell Smith *Towards a world theology: faith and the comparative history of religion*, London: Macmillan, 1980 and *A theology for the world*, SCM, 1986.

40.	For a survey of the history of school worship see John M. Hull *School Worship: an Obituary*, SCM Press, 1975 ch.1.

41. op.cit. p.42.

42. op.cit. pp.122ff.

43. The ILEA Conference (covened 1965) included representatives of the Jewish and Muslim communities, and the Birmingham Conference (convened 1970) included Sikhs and Hindus along with Jews and Muslims. See notes 21 and 25 above.

About the Author

Dr. John M. Hull is Reader in Religious Education in the University of Birmingham School of Education. He is Editor of the *British Journal of Religious Education* and Founder (with a colleague) of the International Seminar on Religious Education and Values. His recent works include *New Directions in Religious Education* (1982), *Studies in Religion and Education* (1984) and *What Prevents Christian Adults from Learning?* (1985).

Birmingham Papers in Religious Education

The aim of this series is to present discussions of issues in religious education to teachers, students, school governors and members of Standing Advisory Councils for Religious Education. Future items in the series will deal in more detail with collective worship and agreed syllabus revision in the light of the 1988 Act.